～ DECORATING ～
WITH
ARCHITECTURAL
DETAILS

~ DECORATING ~
WITH
ARCHITECTURAL
DETAILS

Michael Litchfield

MetroBooks

MetroBooks

An Imprint of the Michael Friedman Publishing Group, Inc.

First MetroBooks edition 2002

Library of Congress Cataloging-in-Publication Data available upon request.

ISBN 1-58663-539-5

Editor: Hallie Einhorn
Art Director: Jeff Batzli
Designer: Lynne Yeamans
Layout: Terry Peterson
Photography Editor: Jennifer Crowe McMichael
Photography Researcher: Samantha Larrance
Production Associate: Camille Lee

Color separations by Fine Arts Repro House Co., Ltd.
Printed in China by C.S. Graphics Shanghai

1 3 5 7 9 10 8 6 4 2

For bulk purchases and special sales, please contact:
Michael Friedman Publishing Group, Inc.
Attention: Sales Department
230 Fifth Avenue
New York, NY 10001
212/685-6610 FAX 212/685-3916

Visit our website:
www.metrobooks.com

TABLE OF CONTENTS

INTRODUCTION

Architectural details provide new ways to think about decorating. When most folks hear the word "decorating," they immediately think of painting and papering, or changing the furniture and drapes. But adding architectural details is an attractive alternative because it is a more piecemeal approach—something you can do a piece at a time without interrupting your life too much or spending exorbitant amounts of money. By introducing trim here, changing a countertop there, or incorporating offbeat objects into a decor, you can animate your living space and give it your own distinct stamp.

One way of introducing details into the home is to turn to manufacturers and retailers who fabricate and sell new moldings, trim, and fixtures. From reproduction plaster rosettes to tony brass spigots, a variety of embellishments can be acquired by approaching these sources. But a more exciting—and often more economic—alternative is presented by the world of architectural salvage. Here you will find trimmings that are one of a kind—embellishments that

Opposite: THIS CLASSICAL TRANSITION FROM COOKING TO DINING AREA IS EFFECTED LARGELY BY TWO HALF-COLUMNS. THE SPACE'S OPEN DESIGN ALLOWS THE EYE TO ROAM FREELY BETWEEN THE TWO ROOMS BEFORE THE BODY ACTUALLY TRAVERSES THE STATELY PASSAGE. NATURAL WOOD, BOOKS, AND A FESTIVE FLOOR KEEP THE TONE LIVELY. Above: NEOCLASSICAL MOLDING THAT RUNS ALONG A ROOM'S EDGE WHERE THE WALL AND CEILING MEET ADDS A TOUCH OF ELEGANCE TO AN OTHERWISE ORDINARY ROOM. WHIMSICAL PAINTED STARS ABOVE AND BELOW CALL ATTENTION TO THIS BEAUTIFULLY CARVED ARCHITECTURAL EMBELLISHMENT, WHILE REVEALING A SENSE OF HUMOR ON THE PART OF THE HOME'S OWNERS.

are as unique as their makers. With architectural salvage, you embark upon an adventure, discovering beautiful and unique details that will add character to your home.

Everyone loves a bargain and the thrill of finding something valuable that has previously gone unnoticed. When you do stumble across that special treasure, you have not only keen eyes and great insight to thank, but good luck—the gift of the gods. There is definitely something alluring and a little magical about finding architectural salvage. Why, for example, does fragile stained glass survive the wrecker's ball when sturdy materials such as concrete and stone are often reduced to rubble? And how is it that shortly after you decided to redo the den, you just happened upon the perfect mantel in a garage up the street?

There is something a little exotic about the pieces themselves, too, as if they have been protected by Fate. Some of the rarer and more expensive materials come from Europe—from grand houses in England, Italy, or France. For these pieces to have traveled such a great distance, somebody clearly smelled a gem in the rough— or a nice profit. But as is often the case, your great find may have traveled from just across town, where one more highway interrupted the slumber of a stately old

Victorian home. Many other pieces of salvage survive by whimsy alone, and each one is sure to have its own individual story.

But why is decorating with architectural artifacts such a hot practice? There are a variety of different answers, depending on who you talk to. Love of a bargain is one possibility. On a more pragmatic level, though, architectural remnants are wonderful for filling holes in the decor that want...something. (You'll know it when you find it.) Hunting for salvage is also a revitalizing antidote to the weekday blahs, drawing you to explore old shops on Saturday morning while most people are still rubbing sleep out of their eyes. Some people purchase salvaged objects as investments to resell later. And others just need something to do with their hands—to fill time and garages.

Larger social forces may be at work, too. People are spending a lot more time at home these days, and while they are not exactly staring at the walls, they are noticing things that might have been overlooked during the go-go eighties. People like their abodes to be appealing retreats, where they can forget their cares and—when possessed with a bit more energy—share who they are with their guests.

The growing trend toward conservation and a lack of tolerance for mindless consumption also come into play. If something is worthwhile, why not save it? Part of that attitude has to do with growing up, of course, for as we mature we seek not only comfort but meaning; a big part of salvage's appeal is that it has a context, some historical significance. It came from someplace; it was part of somebody's life; and now it is part of yours. And like you, it has a story to tell.

Which brings us to the real appeal of salvage: it offers a chance to tell your story, to express yourself. In a time of relentless change, you can build a place where you can be yourself, regardless of what the crazy world outside is doing. And along the way, you will learn a lot.

For one thing, your eye will acquire a great education. Like bird-watching or learning French, the more you practice, the more proficient you become. You will notice architectural details everywhere you go, and you will be able to distinguish great finds from also-rans. Go shopping for ornamental brackets, for example, and on the way home you will find yourself scrutinizing every house on the block for similar details. The more you learn, the richer your world becomes.

Your imagination will also prosper from these outings. Once you have figured out how to obtain more light in that spare bedroom (with some stained glass, perhaps?), you will start ruminating about replacing that tacky kitchen linoleum with fieldstone. It's contagious. You will be surprised at how adept you can become at solving problems; in fact, those troublesome elements of the decor cease to be problems and become a source of fun. Then, when you really get into salvage, you will start looking for trouble, buying oddball objects that go with nothing yet somehow make it all work. The rules go out the window. Sandstone slabs as tabletops? Corrugated tin roofing on the bathroom walls? Why not? Go ahead—spread your wings.

Above: WONDERFUL FOUND FRAGMENTS, NO TWO ALIKE, CHASE EACH OTHER ACROSS A WALL TO FORM A ONE-OF-A-KIND FRIEZE. OFFERING A REFRESHING VISUAL DISTRACTION, THIS UNIQUE EMBELLISHMENT IS AN INVENTIVE ALTERNATIVE TO ORDINARY TRIM.

GLASS

We humans are born loving light—perhaps because we are built that way. Our eyes can see in starlight or sunlight, distinguish seven million different shades of color, change light into nerve signals, and, every second, send a billion pieces of fresh information to our brains.

Is it any wonder, then, that glassmaking is among the most ancient of arts? Glass is a wondrous material: it can change the color of sunlight and permit our eyes to look through walls. And the right window in the right place can certainly change our moods. Hence, glass—stained, leaded, or plain—is an essential tool of any designer.

Once you have found that special piece of glass, get to know it. Hang it over an existing window and observe its colors at different times of day. Put swatches of fabric next to it and think about the interaction of colors and shapes.

Does it suggest an architectural style that is harmonious or contrasting? (Conflicting styles can impart great energy to a home's "active" rooms.) A great window can spawn a whole new look for a decor. And do not forget the more mundane virtues of glass: adding even a small window or a mirror makes a tiny room look bigger; stained glass along a stairway saves electricity and improves safety; and translucent or textured glass admits light to more personal areas, such as bathrooms, without sacrificing privacy.

One of the great boons of searching for that perfect piece of glass is that the quest sharpens the eye, inspiring you to look more closely at everything. You will find yourself walking along streets that you thought you knew, seeing colorful, exquisite architectural details for the first time. Oh, brave new world that has such windows in it!

Opposite: Stained glass is great for setting or fine-tuning a mood. Here, a small recycled piece of stained glass with touches of deep red helps evoke a lush late-Victorian feel, yet at the same time provides a little visual relief from it. Although most everything here is rich in hue, from the cabinets to the trim to the heavy curtains, the elegant floral motif of the stained glass is an airy counterpoint to a dining room that might otherwise be a tad too formal. **Above:** A painted glass beauty such as this, with prismatic jewels around the border, can be put to a multitude of uses. Because it is so heavily figured, this vibrant piece is ideal for transforming a window that currently does not have much of a view. Or the glass could be illuminated from behind and hung on a wall as a piece of glowing art.

Below: SETTING A RESTFUL TONE, SHADES OF BLUE SOFTEN THE UPPER WINDOWS OF THIS ENCLOSED PORCH AND CREATE THE ILLUSION OF AN INDOOR SKY. MEANWHILE, THE WINDOWS THAT ARE CLOSER TO EYE LEVEL REMAIN FREE OF COLOR AND DETAILING SO AS TO PROVIDE A CLEAR VIEW OF THE OUTDOORS. THE BLUE-AND-WHITE COLOR SCHEME OF THE PORCH'S ARCHITECTURAL ELEMENTS IS ECHOED BY THE CHINA PROUDLY DISPLAYED ON DELICATE GLASS SHELVES.

Opposite: ESCHEWING THE TRADITIONAL HEADBOARD, THIS BED IS PLACED UP AGAINST A WALL FEATURING SYMMETRICAL STAINED GLASS WINDOWS THAT BRING WELCOME LIGHT AND COLOR TO THE ROOM. THE YELLOW AND BLUE HUES OF THE GLASS CONTRIBUTE TO THE SPACE'S COUNTRY TONE, WHICH IS FURTHER ENHANCED BY AN AIRY OAK LATTICE INGENIOUSLY MOUNTED ABOVE THE BEDROOM ENTRANCE. THE LATTICE ALSO PREVENTS THE OUTER AREA FROM APPEARING TOO BLAND WHEN THE WHITE POCKET DOORS ARE CLOSED.

Above: THIS TOWERING WALL EXPANSE IS ENLIVENED WITH THE HELP OF A DIAMOND-SHAPED STAINED GLASS WINDOW BEARING AN EXQUISITE ABSTRACT DESIGN. THE SURROUNDING WOODEN BEAMS CREATE AN OFFBEAT—AND SLIGHTLY OFF-CENTER—FRAME THAT CALLS ATTENTION TO THE GLASS ARTWORK BEYOND, LENDING IT AN AIR OF IMPORTANCE.

Opposite: Like spices or scent, the right piece of glass can go a long way. This kitchen dining area is deftly enhanced by leaded windows from the late nineteenth century. With their minimalist display of color, these windows maintain the room's sense of simplicity and allow the decor's rich woodwork to shine through.

Above left: This curved window and its graceful sidelights draw the eye out into the world. Had the window's trim been painted white, it would be far less emphatic; but stripped and stained as it is, the woodwork becomes the perfect frame for an immense and constantly changing canvas. Together, the arching glass and encompassing trim lend the spare loft a classical feel and make an otherwise gray cityscape look like a moment captured in time. **Above right:** Stained glass windows provide a wonderful opportunity for setting a theme. Decked with peppers, squash, corn, grapes, and a colorful fish, these cheery windows brighten up an earth-toned kitchen. To prevent these lively pieces of glass from being dwarfed by the surrounding stonework, the carpenter built up the wood casings around the windows.

Above: When illuminated, shades of honey and amber provide a warm, natural glow that blends in beautifully with the soft luster of wood. This soothing overhead lamp was created by the Greene brothers, turn-of-the-century designers whose aesthetic evolved out of the Arts and Crafts movement. **Opposite:** This Greene brothers fixture filters soft light through its golden tinted glass, creating a peaceful ambience for a relaxing dinner. Shining directly above the dining table, the light is gently reflected by the highly polished mahogany.

Right: THIS DETACHED BATH-HOUSE IN THE RAIN FOREST OF OREGON IS ONE OF THE MOST SERENE PLACES ON EARTH—ESPE-CIALLY LATE IN THE DAY WHEN RARE RAYS OF WINTER SUN FILTER THROUGH THE FIR TREES. A FIRE BURNING IN THE WOODSTOVE, A STEAMING BATH IN THE COMFORT-ABLE OLD CLAW-FOOT TUB, AND A FANCIFUL STAINED GLASS SCENE COMBINE TO CREATE THE PERFECT SPOT FOR PEACE AND REFLECTION. THE WORLD BECOMES A MYSTICAL, MAGICAL PLACE WHEN SEEN THROUGH THIS CONTEMPORARY GLASS CREATION DESIGNED BY TENOLD PETERSON. THIS IS LIVING AS IT SHOULD BE: UNWORRIED AND UNHURRIED.

Above: WHAT CAN BE DONE WITH ONLY A SMALL SECTION OF SALVAGED GLASS? SCULPTOR TENOLD PETERSON SET THE FACETED JEWELS OF AN OLD WINDOW INTO THIS LUMINOUS LEADED GLASS SHADE HE FASHIONED FROM SCRATCH. WHEN STAINED GLASS WINDOWS ARE OUT OF THE QUESTION, A LAMP SUCH AS THIS IS A WONDERFUL WAY OF GRACING A ROOM WITH THE COMBINED BEAUTY OF COLOR AND GLASS.

Above: RUSTIC YET SOPHISTICATED, OPEN YET COZY, THIS BATH IS A STUDY IN CONTRASTS. THE ETCHED-GLASS BULRUSHES BEHIND THE TUB ECHO THE NATURAL WOOD OF THE ROOF TRUSSES AND THE PLANTS REPOSING AROUND THE ROOM. MEANWHILE, THE FLOOR, COUNTER, AND TUB SURROUND HAVE A MORE POLISHED FLAVOR WITH THEIR GRANITE-COLORED WATERPROOF TILE. THE GREAT UNIFIER IS THE SUNLIGHT, WHICH MAKES ITS GRAND ENTRANCE THROUGH AN EXPANSIVE SKYLIGHT, CAUSING THE BRASS TO GLEAM, THE WALLS TO GLOW, AND THE BODY TO REJOICE.

Below: GLASS BLOCKS, POPULAR IN THE 1950S, ARE MAKING A BIG COME-BACK—AND FOR GOOD REASON. THEY ARE PRACTICAL AS WELL AS ATTRACTIVE, AND THEIR TRANSLUCENCE MAKES THEM PARTICULARLY WELL SUITED TO URBAN BATHROOMS WHERE LIGHT, SPACE, AND PRIVACY ARE AT A PREMIUM. ADDING A FLAIR OF FESTIVITY, GLASS BLOCKS CAN PICK UP COLOR FROM TOWELS AND OTHER TRAPPINGS, AS WELL AS BOUNCE BACK LIGHT FROM NEARBY FIXTURES. MORTAR JOINTS BETWEEN THE BLOCKS ADD A BIT OF VISUAL RHYTHM—A WEL-COME RESPITE FROM THE MONOTONY OF SLIDING-GLASS BATH ENCLOSURES.

Above: BEAUTY MEETS PRACTICALITY: THE CLEAR GLASS ABOVE ADMITS SUN FREELY, WHILE THE OPACITY OF THE LOWER PANELS IS PERFECT FOR PRIVACY. PLUS, THE CASEMENT WINDOW CAN BE OPENED TO VENT MOISTURE AFTER A SHOWER.

Opposite: AN ARCHED WINDOW, ITS POINT SOARING UP TO THE SKY, OPENS UP AN ALCOVE, BRINGING LIGHT AND SPACIOUSNESS TO WHAT MIGHT OTHERWISE BE A SHADOWY NOOK. THE SIMPLE PANELING ON EITHER SIDE OF THE WINDOW BLENDS SEAMLESSLY INTO THE REST OF THE ALCOVE, BUT THESE SIDES ARE ACTUALLY SHUTTERS THAT CAN BE CLOSED WHEN PRIVACY IS DESIRED. COLUMNS HIGHLIGHT THE ARCH, THEIR SIMPLE DESIGN PROVIDING THE AREA WITH AN UNDERSTATED ELEGANCE. TOGETHER, THE COLUMNS AND ARCH CREATE THE PERFECT FRAME FOR A MAGNIFICENT ANTIQUE COPPER TUB THAT IS NESTLED WITHIN THE ALCOVE. **Above:** DESPITE ALL THE WARM, LUSTROUS TOUCHES IN THIS FAMILY ROOM, THE UNIQUE PANELED DOOR MAKES A TREMENDOUS IMPACT. WOODEN PANELS HAVE BEEN REPLACED WITH TRANSLUCENT GLASS TO CREATE A PLAYFUL YET ELEGANT LOOK. MOREOVER, THIS CLEVER DOOR TREATMENT ALLOWS LIGHT TO FLOW FROM ONE ROOM TO THE NEXT.

Left top: GLASS CAN BRING A FRESH LOOK TO EXTERIOR DOORS. THE INTENSE DETAILING ON THESE GLASS INSETS PREVENTS OUTSIDERS FROM HAVING A CLEAR VIEW OF THE INTERIOR AND INTRODUCES A TOUCH OF REFINEMENT TO THE RUSTIC FACADE. WITH SUNLIGHT STREAMING IN FROM BEHIND, THESE SAME STUNNING WINDOWS **(left bottom)** CAN BE ENJOYED FROM THE INTERIOR AS THEY SHOW OFF THEIR VIBRANT DESIGNS, CREATING AN UPLIFTING SENSE OF VITALITY. **Opposite:** A DAZZLING DISPLAY OF COLOR AND LIGHT IS CREATED BY THE EXTENSIVE USE OF STAINED GLASS IN THIS HIGHLY ORNATE ROOM THAT HOUSES A DINING AREA, A RELAXED SITTING AREA, AND AN INTIMATE WORK SPACE. WITH ITS GOLDEN HUES AND RADIATING WOODEN BEAMS, THE DYNAMIC STAINED GLASS ARCH AT THE FAR END OF THE ROOM APPEARS AS A GIANT SUN. A FEW SQUARES OF PLAIN GLASS HAVE BEEN INCORPORATED INTO THE CENTER OF THE ARCH TO PERMIT A CLEAR PEEK OUTSIDE. TO FURTHER GIVE THE EYES A REST, PLAIN GLASS IS USED FOR THE FULL-LENGTH WINDOWS OVERLOOKING THE GARDEN, ALLOWING THE SOOTHING GREENERY TO BE ENJOYED FROM WITHIN. TYING IN WITH THE GARDEN THEME, SHADES OF GREEN AND BLUE ARE PREVALENT IN THE STAINED GLASS THAT COVERS THE CEILING. THESE SAME HUES ARE DEFTLY ECHOED IN THE TABLE SETTING BELOW.

WOOD

Wood possesses many beautiful, life-affirming qualities. In its often intricate grain, you can see the route that water once traveled, up from the earth and out through the leaves to the heavens. And though the many lovely colors of wood can be explained by various chemical properties, describing wood's rich glow invariably begs analogies to life itself.

Wood is frequently rich in history. On a hand-hewn beam, you might see the primitive adze marks made by a pioneer who was building a house out of a virgin forest. Or perhaps that ornate casing came from a dusty colonial town in Mexico, from an estate carved out by conquistadors. Suddenly, you feel your place in the continuum of time.

Visually, wood enriches any decor. It is the perfect antidote to vast expanses of Sheetrock or plaster. Carved or heavily figured, wood imparts playfulness and joy; stripped or left in its natural form, it lends a warm, rustic charm; polished so that its highlights shine, it can be formal and elegant; and painted, it can take on a relaxed provincial tone.

Wherever wood appears, it works its magic. Wood trim can tie together the disparate elements of a room, make a nondescript corner special, smooth the transition from one surface to the next, hide unsightly seams, frame a favorite window, or just repose quietly until the next time you notice how beautiful it is. In short, wood has personality.

Opposite: STRIKING RESULTS WERE ACHIEVED IN THIS KITCHEN RENOVATION BY SIMPLY ALTERNATING BANDS OF WOOD WITH WHITE WALLS AND CABINETS. THE EXPOSED BEAMS ECHO THE WIDE PINE FLOORBOARDS, AND THE ARCH AND COUNTERTOPS ARE KINDRED SOULS WITH THE BUTCHER-BLOCK ISLAND. THE FINISHING TOUCH IS THE SHINY ARRAY OF COPPER POTS AND PANS, WHICH REFLECT THE ROOM BACK ONTO ITSELF. **Above:** THIS BRACKET IS NOT PERFORMING ANY STRUCTURAL SERVICE—JUST SITTING PRETTY. ALTHOUGH BRACKETS ARE WONDERFUL FOR SUPPORTING MANTELS, WINDOW SEATS, AND BUILT-IN DESKS, THEY CAN ALSO STAND ON THEIR OWN AS INTRIGUING, EYE-CATCHING EMBELLISHMENTS.

Right: A HEAVENLY SLEEPING ALCOVE—OR IS IT A NAVE? THIS CHURCHLIKE ARCH FITS WONDERFULLY INTO THE TIGHT SPACE, AND THE BRILLIANT COLORS KEEP THE WHOLE ASSEMBLAGE FROM BECOMING TOO STUFFY OR ECCLESIASTICAL. ALONG WITH A LAYER OF RED PAINT, THE ARCH HELPS TO DEFINE THE ALCOVE AS A SEPARATE SPACE WITH A DISTINCT PURPOSE.

Above: IF YOU LOVE ANTIQUES BUT WONDER HOW TO INCORPORATE THEM INTO AN ESSENTIALLY MODERN SPACE, LOOK NO FURTHER. HERE, A HAND-HEWN TIMBER WITH ITS ADZE MARKS STILL SHOWING IS SUCCESSFULLY REBORN AS A MANTEL IN A NEW HOUSE. BECAUSE THE BEAM IS SO MASSIVE AND PRIMITIVE, IT PROVIDES AN OLDER-THAN-THOU CONTEXT FOR ALL THE OTHER PIECES: THE WEATH-ERED GEESE DECOYS, THE ELEGANT CAPTAIN'S CHAIR, AND THE WIDE BOARD TABLE. A CLOCK WITHOUT HANDS IS A PERFECT METAPHOR FOR THE ROOM.

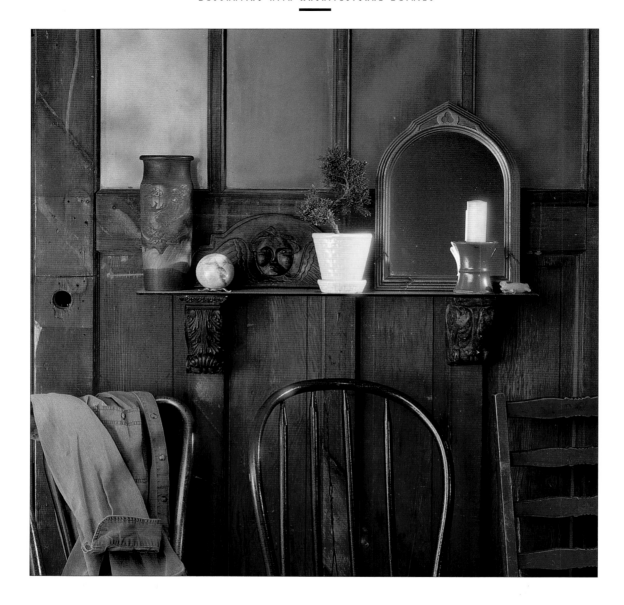

Above: WHEN IS A DOOR NOT A DOOR? WHEN IT'S A WALL. HERE, AN OLD BARN DOOR, WEATHERED AND MELLOW,

FINDS NEW LIFE AS A PARTITION BETWEEN A KITCHEN AND A DINING ROOM. THANKS TO TRANSLUCENT PANELS, AN

ABUNDANCE OF LIGHT PASSES BETWEEN THE TWO ROOMS. BECAUSE THE WOOD WAS A BIT BEATEN UP TO BEGIN WITH, IT

PROVIDES A WORRY-FREE SURFACE TO HANG OBJECTS FROM AND OFFERS A WONDERFUL OPPORTUNITY TO DISPLAY DECORATIVE

PIECES (WHICH ALSO HELP TO COVER UP SOME OF THE ROUGHER SPOTS). FURTHERMORE, THE DOOR SERVES

AS A RELAXED BACKDROP FOR A MOTLEY COLLECTION OF OLD FURNITURE (OR OLD FRIENDS).

Above: THIS ARCH WAS ORIGINALLY PAINTED, BUT BY STRIPPING AND STAINING IT TO MATCH THE OTHER WOOD ELEMENTS IN THE HOUSE, THE DESIGNER TIED THE SPACE TOGETHER VISUALLY. WITH ITS ULTRAWHITE WALLS, THE HOUSE IS EMINENTLY MODERN, BUT THE WOOD WARMS IT AND MAKES IT COMFORTABLE. LIKEWISE, THE BRICK FLOOR HELPS TO CREATE A RELAXED, LOW-MAINTENANCE DWELLING.

Above: ANCIENT GREECE, ANYONE? THE FLUTED WOOD COLUMNS IN THIS SEASIDE RETREAT ARE SIMPLE AND EVOCATIVE, CREATING AN OPEN, AIRY FEELING THAT IS FURTHER INDUCED BY AN IMMENSE WALL MIRROR. WITH ITS POWER OF REFLECTION, THE MIRROR INCORPORATES THE TURQUOISE SEA INTO THE DECOR AND ADDS AN INVIGORATING SPLASH OF COLOR TO THE ROOM'S NEUTRAL PALETTE.

Above: THESE MYTHICAL GRIFFINS ARE THE SORT OF THING YOU BUY ON A WHIM AND THEN PUZZLE OVER FOR YEARS UNTIL YOU FIND JUST THE RIGHT USE FOR THEM. POSSIBILITIES INCLUDE: SERVING AS LEGS TO SUPPORT A PLATE-GLASS COFFEE TABLE; ACTING AS MATCHING POSTS FOR AN ECCENTRIC STAIRWAY; OR GUARDING THE ENTRANCE OF A MAD SCIENTIST'S LABORATORY.

Above: BECAUSE MOST BRACKETS ARE RATHER STYLIZED AND STIFF, THIS ONE IS RARE INDEED. MORE LIKE ONE OF WILLIAM BLAKE'S ANGELS THAN AN ARCHITECTURAL DETAIL, THIS SINUOUS CARVING DESERVES A SPECIAL SPOT. HERE, IT NICELY ADORNS A ROUGH PLASTER ALCOVE.

Left: A SAVVY DESIGNER RESISTED THE TEMPTATION TO CLEAN UP THIS OLD MEXICAN DOOR. CONSEQUENTLY, ITS HISTORY IS TANGIBLE TO ALL WHO ENTER. THE SPARE WHITE WALL FURTHER ACCENTUATES IT, AS IF TO SAY, "HOW MANY LIVES, CONTENT AND DESPERATE, LOVING AND GRIEVING, LIVING AND LEAVING, PASSED THROUGH THIS DOOR IN TWO CENTURIES? AND WHO WILL PASS AFTER YOU?" **Above:** SOMETIMES ARCHITECTURAL ARTIFACTS SURVIVE NOT BECAUSE THEY ARE TERRIBLY FANCY OR VALUABLE, BUT BECAUSE THEY HAVE SOME INEFFABLE SPIRIT OR CHARACTER. FASHIONED FROM MANY SHORT PIECES OF WOOD (BECAUSE LONGER BOARDS WERE DIFFICULT TO OBTAIN), THESE DOORS WERE PROBABLY COMMON WHEN NEW. BUT AS THEY HAVE WARPED AND DEEPENED IN COLOR, THEY HAVE BECOME FOLK ART. TO SHOW THEM OFF TO THEIR GREATEST POTENTIAL, A DESIGNER HAS WISELY SET THEM IN AN EXPANSE OF BUFF-COLORED ADOBE.

Above: OLD WOODEN COLUMNS ARE COMBINED WITH NEW CAPITALS, AN ARCHITECTURAL CANOPY, AND LOW MOLDINGS TO DELINEATE A MAGNIFICENT ENTRANCE. WITH THEIR PEELING PAINT, THE COLUMNS PROVIDE A POWERFUL CONTRAST TO THE SLEEK, POLISHED LOOK OF THE NEWER ARCHITECTURAL ELEMENTS, YET AT THE SAME TIME BLEND IN HARMONIOUSLY WITH THE ANTIQUE FURNISHINGS IN THE AREA BEYOND. ACCENTS OF GOLD ADD SOME SPARKLE TO THE PREDOMINANTLY WHITE SURROUNDINGS. **Opposite:** THE DESIGNER OF THIS ROOM HAD A GREAT EYE AND AN EXQUISITE SENSE OF COLOR. THE GREEN OF THE WAINSCOTING AND THE DEEP YELLOW OF THE WALLS ARE COMMONLY USED IN ARTS AND CRAFTS TILE WORK, AND THEY CONTRAST NICELY WITH THE BLUE CERAMICS AND LAMP SHADE FROM THAT ERA. RICH, DARK WOOD IS AN IMPORTANT PART OF THE PALETTE, AND THE BROWN BAND WITHIN THE CROWN MOLDING IS A DEFT TOUCH.

Above: WITH ITS DEEP REDDISH HUE, THE WOOD USED IN THIS ROOM IMPARTS A LUXURIOUS TONE TO THE OVERALL DECOR. A MULTIFACETED ORNAMENTAL COLUMN EMBELLISHED WITH DARK BANDS THAT GIVE IT ADDED DIMENSION UNITES THE CHERRY WAINSCOTING BELOW AND THE MATCHING MOLDING ABOVE, THEREBY IMBUING A SENSE OF FLUIDITY.

Above: WOODEN BALUSTERS CAN BE USED FOR ALL SORTS OF THINGS, FROM CANDLEHOLDERS TO DESK LEGS. HERE, A RENOVATOR HAS BROUGHT ADDITIONAL WARMTH AND CHARM TO A WOODBURY, CONNECTICUT, HOME BY REUSING SQUAT BALUSTERS TO CREATE A UNIQUE AND ENTICING HEARTH BENCH— GREAT FOR A FIRESIDE CHAT OVER MULLED CIDER.

Opposite: WEATHERED WOODEN PLANKING AND A RUSTIC BALUSTRADE FROM AN OLD PORCH UNITE TO FORM A NOVEL TRANSOM AND GRILLE EFFECT ABOVE THIS DOORWAY, LENDING AN AIR OF AUTHORITY TO THE BEDROOM THAT LIES BEYOND. BALUSTERS BEARING A MORE POLISHED LOOK GRACE THE WOODEN BENCH, FORMING A HANDSOME BACKREST THAT MIRRORS THE BUILT-IN SOFA FRAME OPPOSITE IT. THE VERTICALITY OF THESE ARCHITECTURAL EMBELLISHMENTS IS ECHOED BY THE POSTS OF THE HEADBOARD, VISIBLE THROUGH THE OPEN DOORWAY.

Stone

The world of stone has a lot to offer. Fieldstone, limestone, quartz, tile, marble, sandstone, brick, concrete, soapstone, granite, and cobblestone are all available for you to choose from. Although stone is generally considered to be a hard, inanimate substance, some masons swear it lives; and since most children have seen stones skipping, there may be something to the notion. Granted, none of the materials mentioned above is ever going to read the newspaper, eat spaghetti, or complain about taxes, but when properly employed, stone is remarkably warm, colorful, and—for lack of a better word—alive.

Stone is also the great mixer. Usually of a neutral or subdued color, it coordinates with almost any style, furnishing, rug, or other type of trapping. Because most varieties are relatively impervious to water (porous varieties such as sandstone are not), they are often placed where there is a lot of traffic, moisture, or both. Stone is a natural for outdoor areas, and makes a handsome border for ponds and the like. But the real chemistry occurs between stone and wood: old friends in the wild, they look extraordinarily civilized when paired in your home.

Another match made in heaven is the combination of sunlight and stone. Sunlight is great for revealing all sorts of subtle hues and textures. And, as a special bonus, stone will in turn radiate the sun's warmth long after the sun itself has set.

Opposite: Stone serves as a nice bit of visual punctuation where one room meets another: here, the kitchen begins. By finding a fragment of a Corinthian capital roughly the same height as the cabinets, the designer was able to place a countertop over both, thereby extending the work surface and linking the decorative with the practical. **Above:** Now this is a tub where you can splash to your heart's content with no harm done. Illuminated by diffuse light through translucent glass blocks, the roughly cut stone slabs come across as curiously soft and inviting. The neutral color of the stone allows it to blend in smoothly with the various other materials, fixtures, and colors employed in the decor.

Below: IF FASHION MODELS CAN BE SAID TO HAVE "GOOD BONES," SO CAN COMMODIOUS HOUSES. HERE, EXPOSED FIELDSTONE, HAND-HEWN BEAMS (WITH TRACK LIGHTING HIDDEN AMONG THEM), AND GENEROUS WINDOWS CONSPIRE TO MAKE YOU FEEL WISE AND WELCOME. ALTHOUGH PRESENTLY CASUAL, THIS ROOM COULD HOST ANY ACTIVITY—FROM A FORMAL DINNER TO A BLACK-TIE CONCERT (THE ACOUSTICS WOULD BE FANTASTIC) TO ROUGH-HOUSING WITH THE KIDS. THE POTTED TREES ARE A PLEASANT REMINDER THAT EVERYTHING IN THIS ROOM ONCE LIVED OUTSIDE. **Opposite:** THIS FIREPLACE OF RECYCLED BRICK IS WONDERFULLY FUN BECAUSE THE MASON THUMBED HIS NOSE AT THE USUAL CONVENTION OF NEATLY PLACING BRICKS IN ORDERLY HORIZONTAL ROWS. THE INSPIRING JUMBLE ADDS A LOT OF LIFE AND ENERGY TO A ROOM THAT IS OTHERWISE QUITE CONSERVATIVE.

Above: ALTHOUGH WALK-THROUGH ARCHES ARE USUALLY ELABORATE AF-FAIRS, THIS PARTICULAR ARCH QUIETLY DEFINES A WET BAR, GIVING IT A SUBTLE ELEGANCE. USING STONE OF A SIMILAR COLOR FOR THE CABINET BASE AND BACKSPLASH HELPS TIE THE AREA TOGETHER. WHEN THE SPOTLIGHTS ARE OFF AND THE BAR IS NOT IN USE, THIS CORNER OF THE ROOM RECEDES VISUALLY.

Opposite: IF THIS FIREPLACE WERE A TYPE OF MUSIC, IT WOULD BE A GRAND OPERA. YET AS SPLASHY AND DRAMATIC AS IT IS, IT TOOK A LOT OF PATIENCE AND PERSISTENCE TO COLLECT ALL THESE ELEGANT PIECES—AS WELL AS A LOT OF VISION TO USE THEM SO INGENIOUSLY. IT IS, IN FACT, A WALL OF ART: HERALDIC MEDALLIONS, GRECO-ROMAN MEN, A ROARING BEAST, AND LOVELY FLORAL FRIEZE WORK. THE FLAGSTONE HEARTH WOULD LOOK GREAT WITH A RICHLY FIGURED ORIENTAL RUG LAPPING UP AGAINST IT AND A LEATHER WINGBACK CHAIR OFF TO ONE SIDE.

Above: WE ARE SO USED TO SEEING MASONRY MATERIALS AS WEIGHTY AND FIXED THAT WE FORGET HOW FLUID, VARIABLE, AND ADAPTABLE THEY ARE BEFORE THEY HAVE HARDENED IN PLACE. IN OTHER WORDS, ANYTHING CAN BE SET INTO MASONRY, AS EVIDENCED BY THE INVENTIVE INCORPORATION OF THIS STONE FACADE INTO A BRICK MASS. AN UNEXPECTED ELEMENT SUCH AS THIS CAUSES EVERY OTHER ASPECT OF THE ROOM TO SEEM DYNAMIC, TOO, AS IF IT WERE SUBJECT TO YOUR WHIMS AND WISHES. AND, INDEED, IT IS.

Above: IN THE RIGHT HANDS, STONE, THAT MOST EARTHLY OF MATERIALS, CAN BECOME ALMOST AIRY. HERE, KAREN AND TENOLD PETERSON USED A LIGHT MORTAR TO EMPHASIZE THE SHAPES OF INDIVIDUAL FIELDSTONE PIECES, CLIMAXING IN AN ALMOST BIRDLIKE EXPLOSION OF FORMS OVER THE CENTER OF THE FIREPLACE. THE UNUSUAL-LOOKING CONTRAPTION TO THE RIGHT OF THE MANTEL IS A SALVAGED 1730s PARISIAN MECHANISM THAT, THROUGH A SERIES OF CHAINS, WEIGHTS, GEARS, AND PULLEYS, TURNS A ROTISSERIE SPIT IN THE FIREBOX.

Opposite: THE BOLD USE OF RED ARIZONA SANDSTONE MARKS THIS DINING AREA AS A PLACE WHERE SOMETHING IS GOING TO HAPPEN—GREAT CONVERSATIONS, FANTASTIC FOOD, PEOPLE YOU JUST CAN'T GET ENOUGH OF. TRUE, TABLETOPS ARE SELDOM SO MASSIVE OR IRREGULAR, BUT THEN AGAIN, SURPRISE IS A FIRST COUSIN OF DELIGHT. TOGETHER WITH THE WARM WALL COLORS, THE GAILY PAINTED COLUMNS, THE HANDSOME DARK CABINETS, AND THE UNUSUAL PEAKED DOOR IN THE CORNER, THIS STRIKING DINING SURFACE EVOKES THE FEEL OF A TUSCANY ESTATE. **Above left:** SOFT AND LUMINOUS, THIS SOAPSTONE MANTEL IS THE PERFECT CHOICE FOR A COZY BREAKFAST NOOK. THE STONE'S SMOOTH SURFACE CREATES A GENTLY SOOTHING EFFECT, AND ITS NEUTRAL HUE MAKES IT AN EASY COMPANION FOR VIRTUALLY ANY COLOR OR TEXTURE. BUT BEST OF ALL, THIS TYPE OF STONE HAS WONDERFUL HEAT-RETAINING PROPERTIES: HOURS—SOMETIMES EVEN DAYS—AFTER A FIRE HAS DIED, SOAPSTONE WILL CONTINUE TO RADIATE HEAT. **Above right:** HERE, STONE IS USED MASTERFULLY TO GIVE A SOFT, TIMELESS FEELING TO A HANDSOME KITCHEN AND TO FRAME A WINDBLOWN PINE OUTSIDE. THE KEY ELEMENTS ARE HUE AND LIGHT; THE USE OF A LIGHT-COLORED STONE AVOIDS AN OVERLY WEIGHTY OR OPPRESSIVE EFFECT, WHILE ACCENT LIGHTS BRING OUT DORMANT TEXTURES AND COLORS. THESE WARM HIGHLIGHTS WORK BEAUTIFULLY WITH THE WOODEN KITCHEN CABINETS TO CREATE AN EARTHY TONE.

Opposite: THIS RUSTIC BRICK WALL SERVES AS A POWERFUL BACKDROP FOR AN INTERESTING COLLECTION OF ODDS AND ENDS, INCLUDING A VOTIVE SHELF AND MAGAZINE RACK. IF YOURS IS AN URBAN ROW HOUSE, THERE MAY BE A SIMILARLY HANDSOME EXPANSE OF BRICK BEHIND THAT CHIPPED PLASTER OR DULL DRYWALL. FREE IT! **Above:** WHEN YOU FIND AN ARTIFACT YOU LOVE, SOMETIMES YOU NEED ONLY PUT IT OUTSIDE AND LET NATURE ACCESSORIZE IT FOR YOU. ALTHOUGH THIS TIMELESS BEAUTY ORIGINALLY GRACED AN URBAN FACADE, SHE NOW RESTS EASY ABOVE A GARDEN BENCH, WHERE SHE SERVES AS A QUIET COMPANION FOR THOSE DEEP IN THOUGHT.

Above: WITH A LITTLE IMAGINATION, YOU DO NOT NEED MUCH MONEY. ALL THE MATERIALS HERE ARE COMMONPLACE, BUT BY CREATING A STRONGLY DIAGONAL "CRAZY QUILT" OF GRANITE SQUARES, BRICK, AND MISCELLANEOUS TILE FRAGMENTS, THE DESIGNER ADDED A LOT OF VISUAL INTEREST TO A WALKWAY INTERSECTION. FLOWERS OR TREES CAN BE ADDED LATER BY PULLING UP A FEW SECTIONS OF BRICK.

Right: USING THE MATERIALS AT HAND, MOST NOTABLY SALVAGED COBBLESTONES, ARCHITECT deROY MARK CREATED AN OASIS OF CALM IN THE BACKYARD OF THIS PHILADELPHIA TOWN HOUSE. ANY DECORATIVE TOUCHES ADDED TO AN AREA SUCH AS THIS CAN BE ENJOYED TWICE—AS REFLECTIONS IN THE POND. THE WHOLE EFFECT IS DECIDEDLY FLORAL, A WELCOME COMPLEMENT TO THE SURROUNDING RECTILINEAR BUILDINGS.

A Potpourri of Salvage

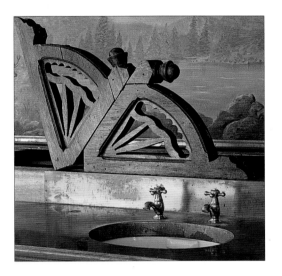

Life can be a fairly predictable affair, so if you want to breathe some freshness and color into it, a good place to start is in the home. Some of the most striking decors stem from unexpected uses of salvaged objects and unusual juxtapositions, so let your imagination run wild. Have fun, and believe in magic.

Salvage can be found in a wide variety of places. Your best friend's garage, the south of France, Omaha, that flea market on the far side of town, and the warehouse district on a Sunday morning are all possible resting places for that special treasure just waiting to be discovered. Your prized find might be something as small as an antique faucet, or it may be a whole claw-foot tub; it may be as basic as a Victorian light fixture or as unusual as a rusty old soda machine.

When you do stumble upon that certain something, try negotiating the price—haggling can be fun.

Then, if you cannot decide what to do with your new acquisition, turn it upside down or sideways. If it is an outside fixture, try putting it in the bedroom or bathroom. A wrought-iron grille from a garden gate can make a beautiful headboard.

One friend makes a party of redecorating. She asks everyone to bring a potluck dish and something strange. Several potlucks later she has a mantel lined with Victorian doorknobs, several large laboratory jars filled with colorful glass shards, and a bathroom wall "papered" with vintage neckties. Although these specific adornments may not appeal to everyone's tastes, the moral of the story is "When in doubt, do the strange."

Opposite: THIS BATHROOM IS PARTICULARLY INVITING BECAUSE SOMEBODY BROKE A FEW RULES. MOST TUBS ARE TUCKED IN A CORNER OR BUILT AGAINST A WALL, BUT HERE A MAGNIFICENT CLAW-FOOT TUB IS THE FOCAL POINT OF THE ROOM, BECKONING THOSE WHO ENTER TO PARTAKE IN A RELAXING, REJUVENATING BATH. THE PAINTED EXTERIOR OF THE TUB IS ANOTHER ODDBALL TOUCH THAT GIVES THIS CHARMING BATHROOM AN ORIGINAL FLAIR. **Above:** IF YOU LIKE THE SHAPE OF SOMETHING, PUT IT WHERE YOU CAN SEE IT. HERE, TWO BRACKETS—PROBABLY FROM THE UNDERSIDE OF A STAIRCASE—REST ON A SHELF BEHIND A HANDSOME COPPER-CLAD BATHROOM SINK. BECAUSE THEY ARE NOT PHYSICALLY ATTACHED TO THE SURFACE, THEY CAN BE MOVED IN ANY NUMBER OF INTERESTING CONFIGURATIONS.

Opposite: THIS EXQUISITE RENOVATION COMBINES TWO SALVAGED ELEMENTS: AN OLD CLAW-FOOT TUB AND A PANELED DOOR CUT DOWN AND REUSED TO CREATE A TUB SURROUND. BOXING IN A CLAW-FOOT IN THIS MANNER SOLVES SEVERAL DESIGN PROBLEMS: IT PROVIDES STORAGE SPACE NEARBY, CREATES A FINISHED CABINET LOOK, DOES AWAY WITH FUNKY VIEWS UNDERNEATH, AND RETAINS HEAT FROM THE BATH. MOREOVER, THIS CLEVER ARRANGEMENT GRACEFULLY HIDES ANY MISSING OR MISMATCHED TUB FEET, A COMMON CHARACTERISTIC OF OLD TUBS.

Right: WHEN COMBINED WITH A MASTERPIECE SUCH AS THIS, A SMALL ASSORTMENT OF FAVORITE OBJETS D'ART SEEMS PERFECTLY AT HOME IN A POWDER ROOM. A VARIETY OF CARVED ELEMENTS, INCLUDING THE CAPITAL OF A COLUMN, IS INGENIOUSLY USED TO SUPPORT A LAVATORY. THE COUNTERTOP FURTHER DEFIES CONVENTION WITH ITS UNUSUAL UNDULATING SHAPE.

Above left: OLD PLUMBING FIXTURES ARE AMONG THE MOST PRIZED PIECES OF SALVAGE BECAUSE THEY OFTEN PREDATE STANDARDIZATION. THIS COMMON BUT ELEGANT TUB FAUCET SET CARRIES WITH IT A SENSE OF TRADITION. THE DROOPING HANDLES AND THE BULBOUS FORMS ARE ALMOST FLUID IN THEMSELVES. **Above right:** THESE BIRD AND RABBIT HANDLES ADD A PLAYFUL TOUCH TO AN OTHERWISE ORDINARY WHITE PORCELAIN SINK AND TILE VANITY. WITH THEIR SILVER SHINE AND INTRICATE LINES, THESE FIXTURES WOULD BE EQUALLY AT HOME ON MODERN AND ANTIQUE SINKS. **Opposite:** THIS OFFBEAT POWDER ROOM IS FILLED WITH SEVERAL UNUSUAL TOUCHES THAT ARE BOUND TO MAKE A LASTING IMPRESSION ON GUESTS. INSTEAD OF BEING EMBEDDED WITHIN A VANITY OR CABINET, A SALVAGED PORCELAIN WASHBASIN IS UNCONVENTIONALLY MOUNTED ON TOP OF AN ELEGANT MARBLE COUNTER, LEAVING THE CHROME PLUMBING FIXTURE BELOW EXPOSED FOR ALL TO SEE. THIS CHROME ELEMENT IS MIRRORED BY THE VERTICALLY MOUNTED TOWEL RACKS USED TO SUPPORT ADJUSTABLE SIDE MIRRORS (ORIGINALLY FROM A TRUCK), PERFECT FOR ADMIRING ONESELF FROM ALL ANGLES. DELICATE CRYSTAL CHANDELIERS HANG OVERHEAD, PROVIDING THE SETTING WITH A FURTHER ELEMENT OF CONTRAST.

Opposite: If you have an area dedicated to meditating or perhaps just being quiet, salvage can help define it and make it special. Here, a painted corner niche with Italian overtones joins with a highly figured wall hanging, river boulders, and a small gilt cabinet to create a serene oasis in a busy world.

Above: Fashioned from an old wooden column, this charming display stand proudly shows off a small array of decorative objects in the midst of an eclectic reading nook.

Above left: THIS WROUGHT-IRON GRILLE, WHICH AT ONE POINT PROBABLY ADORNED THE TRANSOM OF AN EXTERIOR DOOR, NOW SERVES AS A CAPTIVATING DECORATIVE BACKDROP. DESPITE ITS TREMENDOUS PHYSICAL WEIGHT, THE GRILLE SEEMS AIRY, ALMOST LACY, WHEN PAINTED WHITE. SIMILAR GRATING IS USED BENEATH THE GLASS SURFACE OF THE DINING TABLE TO PROVIDE IT WITH A LIVELY PATTERN. **Above right:** THIS ELEGANT CONSOLE TABLE WAS CREATED FROM THE TOP HALF OF AN ORNATE SALVAGED MANTEL. WITH ITS TWISTED-ROPE MOTIF, THE FORMER MANTEL BLENDS IN BEAUTIFULLY WITH THE UPPER PIECES OF THE ENSEMBLE TO EVOKE A FRENCH PROVINCIAL FEELING. **Opposite:** HALLS, HIGH CEILINGS, AND OPEN SPACES NEED NOT BE DULL. HERE, A GOTHIC ROOF FRAGMENT AND A MODERN-LOOKING ARCH JOIN IN WITH A JOYOUS JUMBLE OF PUPPETS, BRACKETS, FAUX STONE, TILE, HOPI FIGURINES, AND BOOKS TO CREATE A SPIRITED DECOR THAT EXUDES ENERGY. BY ENGULFING THE ROOM FROM FLOOR TO CEILING, THESE FASCINATING DECORATIVE OBJECTS KEEP THE EYE MOVING FROM LEVEL TO LEVEL.

Opposite: GENERALLY, "ANYTHING GOES" WHEN USING SALVAGE. BUT WHEN A HOUSE IS AS RICH IN ARCHITECTURAL DETAILS AS THIS LOS ANGELES MANSION, IT IS IMPORTANT TO USE PIECES THAT ARE APPROPRIATE. HERE, AN ORIGINAL FORTUNY FIXTURE HELPS TO SET A MAJESTIC TONE IN A GRAND FOYER. SKILLFULLY CARVED DETAILS GIVE THE ILLUSION THAT THE STATELY LIGHT FIXTURE IS ACTUALLY BEING SUSPENDED BY THICK, OPULENT BANDS OF TWISTED ROPE. **Above left:** SOMETIMES JUST TURNING AN OBJECT NINETY DEGREES CREATES A SINGULAR VISUAL EFFECT. HERE, AN ETCHED CEILING SHADE IS USED AS A SCONCE, AFFIXED TO A THREADED POST COMING STRAIGHT OUT OF THE WALL. GILT AND RECURRENT DIAGONALS ON THE WALL BEHIND ADD TO THE DRAMA, CREATING A LUMINOUS BACKDROP FOR THE STILL LIFE ATOP THE TABLE. **Above right:** LIGHT FIXTURES ARE ALL THE MORE IMPRESSIVE WHEN NEARBY DECORATIVE DETAILS ARE DESIGNED TO MATCH. HERE, THE SWIRLING FLUIDITY OF THIS DELICATE VICTORIAN LIGHT FIXTURE (WHICH MAY HAVE STARTED OUT AS A GAS FIXTURE) IS ECHOED BY THE LACY EMBOSSED PATTERNS OF THE WALL COVERING THAT LIES BEHIND IT.

Above: THERE WAS A TIME WHEN PEOPLE MOVED AROUND A LOT LESS AND THUS NOTICED, AS WELL AS APPRECIATED, DETAIL IN THE LEAST EXPECTED PLACES. THESE TURN-OF-THE-CENTURY BRASS DOOR TRIMMINGS GLADDEN THE EYE, HAVE A PLEASANT HEFT IN THE HAND, AND PAIR UP MAGNIFICENTLY WITH DARK WOOD. **Opposite:** SLEEK ELEVATOR DOORS FROM A MEDICAL BUILDING WERE THE PERFECT FINISHING TOUCH FOR A DOCTOR'S CONTEMPORARY BEDROOM. HIGHLY POLISHED, THEY NOW SERVE AS ELEGANTLY FLUTED CLOSET DOORS THAT BLEND IN SEAMLESSLY WITH THE SILVER-TONED HIGH-TECH ENTERTAINMENT CENTER THEY FLANK.

Above: THIS STUNNING BED IS TRULY A WORK OF ART, MASTERFULLY BRINGING TOGETHER ALL SORTS OF WONDERFUL ARCHITEC-TURAL ELEMENTS. TWO WROUGHT-IRON GRILLES THAT FORMERLY ADORNED GARDEN ENTRANCES HAVE BEEN TRANSFORMED INTO A BREATHTAKING FOOTBOARD AND HEADBOARD THAT COORDINATE BEAUTIFULLY WITH ONE ANOTHER DESPITE THEIR SEPARATE PASTS. FANCIFUL EMBELLISHMENTS GRACE THE POSTS ON EITHER SIDE OF THE HEADBOARD, WHILE DISTINCT SALVAGED FINIALS TOP OFF THOSE FLANKING THE FOOT OF THE BED.

Right: The many found objects that adorn this room, such as a weathered cabinet and two colorful painted shutters, are united only by their owner's eclectic taste and love of a bargain. A veritable work-in-progress, the decor is everchanging as new treasures move in and others are relocated. The neutral colors of the floor and trim readily embrace any and all decorative objects, regardless of their hues or textures. Moreover, these subdued tones allow the room's furnishings and accoutrements to take center stage. **Below:** This little bit of "street theater" shows how easy it is to bring the beauty of the outdoors into a home's interior. Two handsome "wave-slat" shutters screwed to the wall, a tub of geraniums, and...voilà! Your outside is in!

Below: These two recycled exterior columns create a whimsical mock-heraldic entrance to the room beyond, while bas-relief figures over the passageway complete the classical picture. If you are not lucky enough to find an old relief, a new thermoplastic mold can be affixed to the wall and painted to mimic plaster.

Above: Small touches can be delightful, especially ones that introduce new perspective to run-of-the-mill objects. This shelf, perfect for displaying a few of one's favorite things, was formerly a desk drawer. Leftover bits of paint on the bottom lend character and charm.

Opposite: Has Grandma's silver ever been in more elegant company? Someone had a lot of fun repainting the lawn chairs and dragging this old Coke machine into the dining room. And the elaborate, slightly funereal mirror behind adds to the mock formality of it all.

APPENDIX: SALVAGE TIPS

Before your fancy takes flight, here are a few earthly suggestions about finding, buying, and reusing salvage. Mostly, these helpful tips are just plain common sense.

• **Finding it.** Architectural salvage is all over the place, but the more fixed up and refurbished it is, the more it will cost. The obvious places to start are salvage emporiums, warehouses, or yards—check the phone book for listings. Flea markets are good sources for smaller pieces, as are auctions. Construction tradespeople often save architectural remnants: if you know any contractors, tell them what you are looking for. This holds true for architects and antique dealers, too, though they are more inclined to be pricey. If you're adventurous, you can approach a demolition crew at work, but because such sites are dangerous, you may get the brush-off. If you're clear about what you want, though, and have a little cash handy, they may oblige you.

• **Buying it.** Everything is negotiable. If the price of a refurbished item is too high, ask if there are similar pieces "as is," for they should cost less.

• **Moving it.** If your prized find is heavy, give the seller ten or twenty bucks to haul it to your place; it's cheaper than a new automobile seat cover or back surgery. If you do carry the treasure home yourself, always bend your knees when you lift. Likewise, if you tie your weighty find to a roof rack, use rope or tiedown straps. Do not resort to "heavy" string, baling twine, or anything else not up to the job. Looking into the rearview mirror and seeing your new stained glass door scattered across three lanes of swerving cars is no fun.

• **Reusing it.** If you are putting old plumbing or electrical fixtures back into commission, have them checked out by a plumbing or electrical-parts supply house first—or by an appropriate tradesperson. Although safety is your main concern, such suppliers can also be wonderful sources for those tiny little screws and odd-size fittings that hold everything together. And if you are thinking of putting salvaged masonry in a place where it could fall and hurt someone—say, setting a stone capital into a brick wall—you should hire a mason to do it. Choosing the correct mortar and supporting the piece while the mortar dries are best handled by professionals.

Those few suggestions aside, go for it. With a few well-chosen pieces of salvage here and there, your house will be more interesting, more lively, and more creative—in short, more like you.

Sources

SOURCES

ARCHITECTURAL SALVAGE

Architectural Antiques
  Exchange
715 North Second Street
Marion, PA 19123
(610) 664-4559

Architectural Antiques, Ltd.
812 Canyon Road
Santa Fe, NM 87501
(505) 982-0042

Architectural Artifacts, Inc.
4325 North Ravenswood
Chicago, IL 60613
(312) 348-0622

The Brass Knob
2311 18th Street NW
Washington, DC 20009
(202) 332-3370

The Emporium
2515 Morse Street
Houston, TX 77019
(713) 528-3803

Gargoyles, Ltd.
512 South Third Street
Philadelphia, PA 19147
(215) 629-1700

Great Gatsby's Auction Gallery
5070 Peachtree Industrial
  Boulevard
Atlanta, GA 30341
(800) 428-7297

Queen City Architectural
  Salvage
P.O. Box 16541
Denver, CO 80216
(303) 296-0925

Salvage One
1524 South Sangamon
Chicago, IL 60608
(312) 733-0098

DESIGNERS

(page 6)
Shope, Reno, Wharton,
  architects
Greenwich, CT
(203) 869-7250

(page 7)
Kennedy-Wilson International
Santa Monica, CA
(310) 314-8400

(page 11)
Gargoyles, Ltd.
Philadelphia, PA
(215) 629-1700

(page 12, left)
Glass by David Wilson Design
South New Berlin, NY
(607) 334-3015

(page 12, right)
Benn Theodore
Benn Theodore, Inc.
Boston, MA
(617) 227-1915

(page 14)
Larry Bogdanow
Bogdanow and Associates,
  Architects
New York, NY
(212) 966-0313

(pages 15, right and 45, right)
Mary Ann Hall
Hall Design Associates
Denver, CO
(303) 839-9395

(pages 18, 19, and 43, right)
Tenold Peterson
Tenold Peterson Studios/Fine
  Glass Art
Junction City, OR
(503) 998-2750

(page 20)
Madeline Gesser
Hewlett Harbor, NY 11557
(516) 374-7821

(pages 23, 29, and 40, right)
Charles Riley
New York, NY
(212) 473-4173
Los Angeles, CA
(213) 931-1134

(page 24, left and right)
Scott Wylie
Springfield, OR
(503) 741-8385

(page 31, left)
Bob Patino
Patino Limited
New York, NY
(212) 355-6581

(page 32, left)
Carlson Chase Associates
Los Angeles, CA
(213) 969-8423

(page 34)
Peter Wheeler
P.J. Wheeler Associates
Boston, MA
(617) 426-5921

(page 36, left)
Nanticoke Associates
New York, NY
(212) 925-3611

(pages 38 and 46)
Karen Linder
New York, NY
(212) 598-0559

(page 39)
Stephenson's Construction
Attleboro, MA
(508) 222-8191

(page 40, left)
Michele Lewis, architect
Lewis and Gould
New York, NY
(212) 807-6588

(pages 42 and 43, left)
Adolf deRoy Mark, architect
Carefree, AZ 19106
(602) 488-2216

(page 45, left)
Charlotte Forsythe
Mary Prentiss Inn
Cambridge, MA
(617) 661-2929

(page 53)
Mark A. Polo
Polo, M.A. Inc.
Fort Lee, NJ
(201) 224-0322

(page 57)
Cheryl and Jeffrey Katz
C+J Katz Studio, Inc.
Boston, MA 02114
(617) 367-0537

(page 63)
Vince Lattuca
Visconti & Company, Ltd.
New York, NY
(212) 758-2720

(page 65, top)
Richard Kazarian
Richard Kazarian Antiques
Providence, RI
(401) 331-0079

PHOTOGRAPHY CREDITS

©William Abranowicz: p. 15 left; Design: Hall Design Associates; pp. 15 right, 45 right; Design: Judy Prouty: p. 66 right

©Grey Crawford: pp. 35, 51

©Daniel Eifert: Design: Bogdanow & Associates, Architects: p. 14

©Philip Ennis: p. 21 right; Design: Visconti & Company, Ltd.: p. 63

©Tria Giovan: pp. 22, 29, 40 right; Design: Michael Foster: p. 28

©Mick Hales: Design: Patino Limited: p. 31 left

©Rosmarie Hausherr: pp. 11, 18, 19, 24 (both), 27, 32 right, 33 right, 36 right, 42, 43 (both), 47, 48, 49, 54, 62 right

©Nancy Hill: Design: Madeline Gesser, courtesy of *House Beautiful's Home Remodeling and Decorating Magazine*, The Hearst Corporation: p. 20; Design: Nanticoke Associates: p. 36 left; Design: Stewart Witt: p. 21 left

©Bathazar Korab: pp. 61 right, 62 left

©Tim Lee: pp. 44, 50

©Richard Mandelkorn: Design: Kennedy-Wilson International: p. 7

INDEX